S0-ARL-210

7·98

To: Mom

From: Mike, Carol.

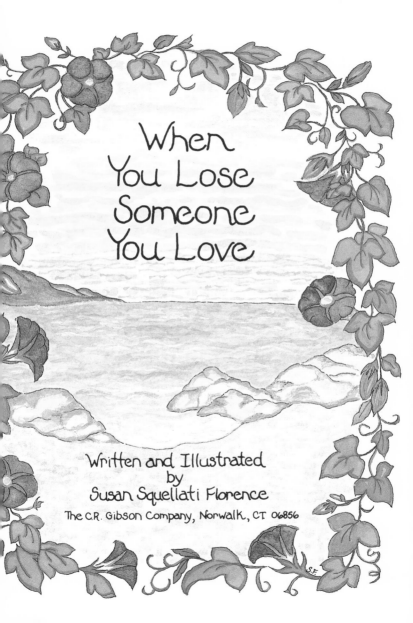

When You Lose Someone You Love

Written and Illustrated
by
Susan Squellati Florence

The C.R. Gibson Company, Norwalk, CT 06856

When someone
you love dies,
a part of yourself
dies too.

For as much as
the one you loved
did not belong to you,

your heart
belonged to them.
You were a part
of each other.

There is a physical hurt
within you.

It is as real
as the emptiness
that surrounds you.

You will wonder
how you will walk
in a world
that no longer holds
the footprints
of your loved one.

You will wonder
how the world can go on
when your world
has stopped.

You will speak silently
in the language of tears,
as your heart
seeks to understand
what it cannot.

Spiritual thoughts,
religious beliefs,
and philosophy
may not take away
the hurt.

SUSAN FLORENCE

But the power
of love
will comfort you.

FLORENCE

Love will be found
in the hearts of those
who surround you
and care about you.

People who have been
in the place of sadness
where you are now,
will be there for you.

The sun
will continue to rise
and the moon
and the stars
will still light
the heavens.

S.F.

You will begin
the sacred
daily ritual
of "remembering".

Your grief will become
your traveling companion...
the part of you
that is compassionate,
and strong, and deep.

In your suffering
you will be given
the greatest challenge
you will ever have ...

S.F.

to be able to accept
what life gives,
and what life
takes away.

Peace will come
to your days
as you begin
to live again
accepting the mysteries
that are a part of life.

With time...
the veil of sorrow
will lift,
and you will see

what is most precious
and most sacred
is the love we share
with the ones we love.

Peace will come
to your heart
and you will know
this love
is an eternal gift.

This love

es forever.

By Susan Squellati Florence

Friendship Is A Special Place
Babies Take Us On A Special Journey
A Book Of Loving Thoughts
Be All That You Are
The Heart of Christmas
A Gift Of Time
Your Journey
With Friends
Hope Is Real
Good Thoughts
A Wedding Wish
When You Lose Someone You Love